Chisholm

by Ian Andsell

D1353513

Lang**Syne**

PUBLISHING

WRITING *to* REMEMBER

LangSyne

PUBLISHING

WRITING *to* REMEMBER

Vineyard Business Centre,
Pathhead, Midlothian EH37 5XP
Tel: 01875 321 203 Fax: 01875 321 233
E-mail: info@lang-syne.co.uk
www.langsyneshop.co.uk

Design by Dorothy Meikle
Printed by Ricoh Print Scotland
© Lang Syne Publishers Ltd 2010

ISBN 978-1-85217-099-8

Chisholm

SEPT NAMES INCLUDE:
Cheseholm
Chisholme
Chisolm

Chisholm

MOTTO:
Feros Ferio
(I am Fierce With The Fierce).

CREST:
A Right Hand Holding a Dagger
Transfixing a Gold Boar's Head.

TERRITORY:
Roxburghshire and
later Inverness-shire.

Chapter one:

The origins of the clan system

by Rennie McOwan

The original Scottish clans of the Highlands and the great families of the Lowlands and Borders were gatherings of families, relatives, allies and neighbours for mutual protection against rivals or invaders.

Scotland experienced invasion from the Vikings, the Romans and English armies from the south. The Norman invasion of what is now England also had an influence on land-holding in Scotland. Some of these invaders stayed on and in time became 'Scottish'.

The word clan derives from the Gaelic language term 'clann', meaning children, and it was first used many centuries ago as communities were formed around tribal lands in glens and mountain fastnesses.

The format of clans changed over the centuries, but at its best the chief and his family held the land on behalf of all, like trustees, and the ordinary clansmen and women believed they had a blood relationship with the founder of their clan.

There were two way duties and obligations. An inadequate chief could be deposed and replaced by someone of greater ability.

Clan people had an immense pride in race. Their relationship with the chief was like adult children to a father and they had a real dignity.

The concept of clanship is very old and a more feudal notion of authority gradually crept in.

Pictland, for instance, was divided into seven principalities ruled by feudal leaders who were the strongest and most charismatic leaders of their particular groups.

By the sixth century the 'British' kingdoms of Strathclyde, Lothian and Celtic Dalriada (Argyll) had emerged and Scotland, as one nation, began to take shape in the time of King Kenneth MacAlpin.

Some chiefs claimed descent from

ancient kings which may not have been accurate in every case.

By the twelfth and thirteenth centuries the clans and families were more strongly brought under the central control of Scottish monarchs.

Lands were awarded and administered more and more under royal favour, yet the power of the area clan chiefs was still very great.

The long wars to ensure Scotland's independence against the expansionist ideas of English monarchs extended the influence of some clans and reduced the lands of others.

Those who supported Scotland's greatest king, Robert the Bruce, were awarded the territories of the families who had opposed his claim to the Scottish throne.

In the Scottish Borders country - the notorious Debatable Lands - the great families built up a ferocious reputation for providing warlike men accustomed to raiding into England and occasionally fighting one another.

Chiefs had the power to dispense justice

and to confiscate lands and clan warfare produced a society where martial virtues - courage, hardiness, tenacity - were greatly admired.

Gradually the relationship between the clans and the Crown became strained as Scottish monarchs became more orientated to life in the Lowlands and, on occasion, towards England.

The Highland clans spoke a different language, Gaelic, whereas the language of Lowland Scotland and the court was Scots and in more modern times, English.

Highlanders dressed differently, had different customs, and their wild mountain land sometimes seemed almost foreign to people living in the Lowlands.

It must be emphasised that Gaelic culture was very rich and story-telling, poetry, piping, the clarsach (harp) and other music all flourished and were greatly respected.

Highland culture was different from other parts of Scotland but it was not inferior or less sophisticated.

Central Government, whether in London

"The spirit of the clan means much to thousands of people"

or Edinburgh, sometimes saw the Gaelic clans as a challenge to their authority and some sent expeditions into the Highlands and west to crush the power of the Lords of the Isles.

Nevertheless, when the eighteenth century Jacobite Risings came along the cause of the Stuarts was mainly supported by Highland clans.

The word Jacobite comes from the Latin for James - Jacobus. The Jacobites wanted to restore the exiled Stuarts to the throne of Britain.

The monarchies of Scotland and England became one in 1603 when King James VI of Scotland (1st of England) gained the English throne after Queen Elizabeth died.

The Union of Parliaments of Scotland and England, the Treaty of Union, took place in 1707.

Some Highland clans, of course, and Lowland families opposed the Jacobites and supported the incoming Hanoverians.

After the Jacobite cause finally went down at Culloden in 1746 a kind of ethnic cleansing took place. The power of the chiefs was curtailed. Tartan and the pipes were banned in law.

Many emigrated, some because they wanted to, some because they were evicted by force. In addition, many Highlanders left for the cities of the south to seek work.

Many of the clan lands became home to sheep and deer shooting estates.

But the warlike traditions of the clans and the great Lowland and Border families lived on, with their descendants fighting bravely for freedom in two world wars.

Remember the men from whence you came, says the Gaelic proverb, and to that could be added the role of many heroic women.

The spirit of the clan, of having roots, whether Highland or Lowland, means much to thousands of people.

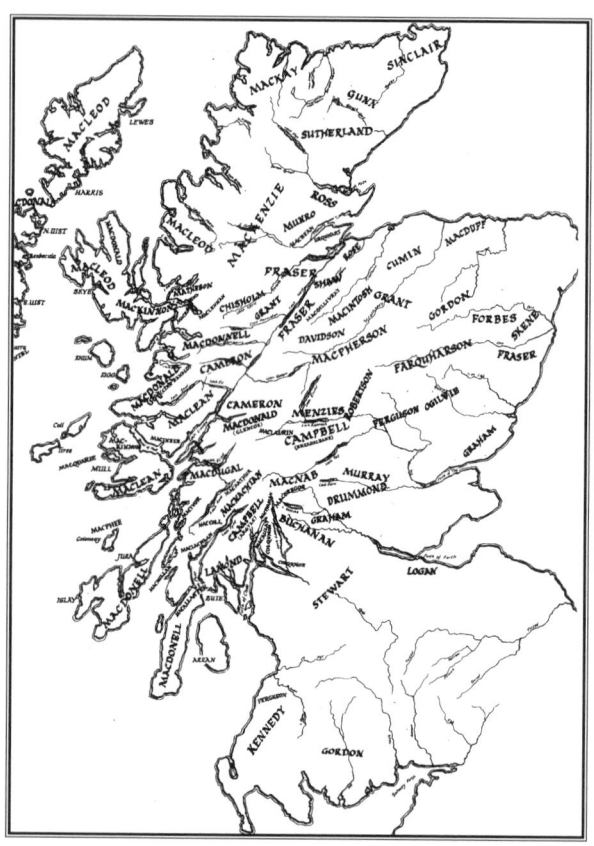

A map of the clans' homelands

Chapter two:

The journey north

In 1066, it is said, the forebear of all the Chisholms landed near Hastings with William the Bastard of Normandy on his mission to conquer England. Nearly a millennium later, his descendants would gather from continents as yet undiscovered to celebrate their kinship on wind-swept hillsides from which their more immediate forebears had been treacherously ejected by the clan's own chief.

What William's companion called himself is not known, but it is likely that his family was granted lands in the Borders during the twelfth century and their name first appears in documents from a hundred years later. Alexander de Chesholme witnessed a charter in 1248, while John de Chesehelme is mentioned in a Bull of Pope Alexander IV dated 1254.

The Barony of Chieseholme lay in the parish of Roberton, Roxburghshire, and it is believed that the word Chisholm meant, in the ancient Beornician language, the 'waterside meadow good for producing cheese'. This pastoral connection is in contrast to the boar's head which has been borne proudly at the centre of the clan's coat of arms since at least 1292 - an association with ferocity which was to be proved appropriate in succeeding centuries.

John de Cheshelme's grandson, Sir John de Chisholme of Berwick, fought at Bannockburn in 1314, on the side of Robert the Bruce. However, the drama of the Chisholm story unfolded not in the Borders, where the family continued for many years, but in the Highlands, where it flourished.

The northern connection began in 1359 when Robert Chisholm became Royal Constable of Castle Urquhart in succession to his mother's father, Sir Robert Lauder of the Bass. Situated on Loch Ness, Urquhart held the strategic key to the Great Glen, that fissure which divides Scotland from Fort William in the west to Inverness in the north east. Robert's authority was subsequently increased when he became Sheriff of Inverness and Justiciar of the North, while his inheritance included lands in Moray, near Elgin and Nairn.

The Chisholm line continued in its original homelands through Robert's youngest son, some of whose descendants also founded the Perthshire branch of the family in Cromlix. But the northern estates increased greatly when Robert's eldest son Alexander married Margaret, daughter of Wiland of the Aird, and thus became the owner of estates in five counties as well as proprietor of his bride's home, Erchless Castle. Clan Chisholm had been founded.

Chapter three:

Land of their fathers

The Erchless Castle which can now be seen in Strathglass, about ten miles west of Beauly, was built between 1594 and 1623, when the chief was John Chisholm, Commissioner of the Peace for Inverness-shire. Nigel Tranter described it as a "handsome tower-house" - a tall, L-shaped four-storey building with turrets, crowstepped gables, harled and whitewashed walls pierc-ed by gunloops and shot-holes.

A Miss Sinclair, writing in the 1800s, said of it: "This place is beauty personified, and you would fall in love with it at first sight. The castle is a venerable white-washed old tower, so entirely surrounded by a wreath of hills that the glen seems scooped out on purpose to hold the house and park."

By 2003, it had become possible for any-one with enough money to enjoy Erchless, for the three-storey nineteenth century north wing of the castle could be rented for between £2,000 and £3,000 per week.

But that is to anticipate a long story. As the Chisholm family settled in the north it acquired Strathglass and Ard, and later came into the estate of Comar, which made them proprietors of a large part of Ross-shire.

Boundaries were fluid in those days, however. On one occasion, Chisholm tenants and those of the Earl of Seaforth in Kintail were in disagreement over the hilly border between their Chiefs' estates. The Chiefs themselves, who were related and on friendly terms, decided on what seemed a peaceful solution to the dispute. An old dairymaid from Kintail walked out from Caisteal Donnan on the Seaforth side, while a Strathglass maid set off from Beinnvean representing the Chisholms. The point where they met was to be recognised as the boundary line.

Unfortunately, when the two confronted each other west of Glen Affric on a hillock between Loch-a-bheallaich and Altbeatha, tempers frayed.

"You have come too far towards Kintail and I will go still further towards Strathglass," the Seaforth dairymaid is reported to have said. The Chisholm maid retorted that if she dared to go a step further it would be the worse for her.

The Seaforth woman stubbornly ignored her and walked ahead, whereupon, according to an old account, "her adversary dealt her a fatal blow with her staff. Thrusting the staff in the ground near the lifeless body, the maid from Strathglass marched in triumph back to Comar."

In keeping with the robust attitudes of the period, all present agreed that the matter had been settled in a satisfactory fashion and the place where the confrontation occurred became known as Cnoc-a-Chuaille or the 'Hillock of the Bludgeon'.

Chapter four:

Alarms and excursions

These were also times when one's neighbours' ox was not only coveted, but might well be spirited away if the night was dark enough. According to a record of 1489, a raid by Wiland Chisholm of Comar and others carried off 56 oxen, 60 cows, 300 sheep, 80 swine, and 15 horses belonging to Hugh Rose of Kilravock.

Nor was pilfering restricted to livestock. One of the Chisholm chiefs, it is said, carried off the daughter of Clan Fraser's chief and hid her on an island on Loch Bruaich. Her father's forces discovered the hiding place but during the struggle which followed the girl was accidentally killed by her own brother. The incident became the subject of a well-known Gaelic song and the burial mounds of those who fell in the battle could still be seen a century ago.

Sadly, Highlanders were no strangers to

the barbarism of witch-hunting. In 1662, accusations of witchcraft against some Strathglass women led to complaints that the investigating commissioners "most cruelly and barbarously tortured the women by waking, hanging them up by the thumbs, holding the soles of their feet to the fire, burning of them, and drawing of others at a horse's tail, binding them with withes about the neck and feet and carrying them so alongst on horseback to prison, whereby, and by other torture, one of them became distracted, another of them removed by death, and all of them have confessed whatever they were pleased to demand of them."

During this time of consolidation of the Chisholms' position in the Highlands, a second legend arose about the adoption of the boar on the clan's arms. The earlier story told that a Chisholm had saved the life of a Scottish king who was attacked by a boar while hunting.

However, according to the alternative version: "The popular tradition is that two brothers determined to destroy a ferocious boar which kept the whole of Strath in constant terror. Having discovered his den, one of the men, as the animal was about to attack him, thrust his hand down its throat, and dragging out the tongue and stomach, his companion exclaimed, "SiSalaich" meaning that he made a filthy grasp. From this comes Si'sal and the brothers became the armorial supporters."

Sure enough, the Highland Chisholms have been known as Siosal ever since.

Chapter five:

Jacobites and the Great Betrayal

During the 1685 rebellion the Chisholm stronghold, Erchless Castle, was defended stoutly but unsuccessfully by the Jacobite John Chisholm against General Livingstone, commander-in-chief of the Scottish forces of William of Orange. In the build-up to the Jacobite Rising of 1715 John's son Roderick offered his services to King George I. Bizarrely, his overtures were rejected, so Roderick led 200 of his clan to Sherrifmuir in the cause of the Old Pretender.

Following defeat, his estates were forfeited but later restored after he was pardoned in 1735. However, Roderick came out for Bonnie Prince Charlie in 1745 and led 80 Chisholms through the campaign until Culloden, where his son, also Roderick, and 30 clansmen were killed.

The nineteenth century spelled the end of the Chisholms' glory years, as it did for so many other clans. The cause - clan chiefs populating the hillsides with sheep instead of their own clansmen. Alexander, the 23rd chief of Clan Chisholm, resisted the trend but his successors ensured that the clearances from the Chisholm heartland of Strathglass were among the worst in the Highlands.

Alexander's son William began the work in 1801 and it is said that half of the clan was evicted within a year, with many sailing for Canada and Nova Scotia. Estimates suggest that more than 10,000 Strathglass clansfolk were evicted or emigrated from 1801-1809. William's own son Alexander - educated at Cambridge like many of his peers - continued the grim work and almost completely depopulated the strath.

One of the few survivors, the Gaelic bard Donald Chisholm, said: "Our chief is losing his kin. He prefers sheep in the glens, and his young men away in the camp of the army."

Ironically, some members of the clan in

exile perpetuated its name through their exploits, particularly in America.

Jesse Chisholm was born in East Tennessee about 1806 with a father of Scots extraction and a Cherokee Indian mother. A hunter, guide, scout and pathfinder, he traded and lived with Comanches, Kiowas and Creeks. In 1865 Jesse led a wagon train from a settlement near Abilene in Kansas to San Antonio, Texas - a cattle-droving route which was known forever after as the Chisholm Trail.

Coincidentally - and confusingly - two years later John Chisum blazed the historic Chisum Trail when he drove 900 head of cattle from Paris, Texas, across the desert then north to the Pecos Valley in southeastern New Mexico.

Chapter six:

Reunited

All the upheavals of the early nineteenth century were for nothing, for the main line of the family ended in 1838. In 1887, following the death of the then Chief, Roderick, without a male heir, the chiefship and the clan land were separated and passed through two separate female lines. A line of Border Chisholms died out in 1899, when Colonel John James Scott Chisholme of Stirches was killed in South Africa during the Boer War. The final humiliation for the Highland branch came in 1937, with the sale of the estates and Erchless Castle.

But the history of the Chisholms was far from over. In 1951, the Clan Chisholm Society was founded and at the beginning of a new millennium, in July 2001, the Society held a seven-day clan gathering to mark its 50th anniversary. Chisholms travelled from the USA, Australia, Canada, France, New Zealand, South Africa and all over Britain to visit the land of their forebears and to meet cousins from afar.

Two ceremonies were held to provide permanent memorials of the occasion. On a cairn erected by the Clan Chisholm Society in 1968 overlooking the village of Cannich, a bronze plaque provided by the Society's Canadian branch was unveiled by the head of the clan, The Chisholm. Inscribed on it in Gaelic and English was an old Highland proverb, 'Cuimnichaibh air na daoine', which translates as *'Remember the people from whom you have come'*.

Later, The Chisholm unveiled a second plaque made of black granite and mounted by Nova Scotia Chisholms on another cairn on the shore of Loch Mullardoch in Glen Cannich. The wording on this plaque read: 'Two centuries after the diaspora of the Chisholms from Strathglass, their descendants returned from five continents to the lands of their origin, now devoid of the Chisholm name, to confirm their heritage'.

It was an eloquent end to a long chapter in a people's history, made more poignant by the ancient Celtic blessing given on both occasions by the Rev. Dr. Francis Chisholm:

> *Deep peace of the running wave to you*
> *Deep peace of the flowing air to you*
> *Deep peace of the quiet earth to you*
> *Deep peace of the shining stars to you*
> *Deep peace of the gentle night to you.*

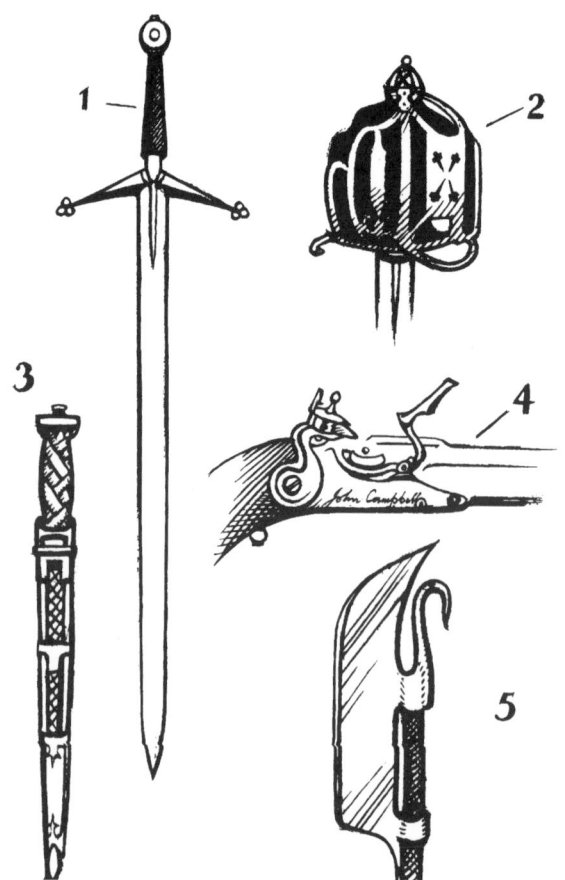

Highland weapons

1) The claymore or two-handed sword
(fifteenth or early sixteenth century)

2) Basket hilt of broadsword
made in Stirling, 1716

3) Highland dirk
(eighteenth century)

4) Steel pistol *(detail)* made in Doune

5) Head of Lochaber Axe as carried
in the '45 and earlier